THE
GREAT CENTENNIAL

Text and Photography by Les MacLean

The Great Centennial
Copyright © 2019 by Les MacLean

All rights reserved. No part of this publication may be reproduced, distributed, or transmitted in any form or by any means, including photocopying, recording, or other electronic or mechanical methods, without the prior written permission of the publisher or author, except in the case of brief quotations embodied in critical reviews and certain other noncommercial uses permitted by copyright law.

Although every precaution has been taken to verify the accuracy of the information contained herein, the author and publisher assume no responsibility for any errors or omissions. No liability is assumed for damages that may result from the use of information contained within.

LOC: 2019941054

Paperback: 978-1-950073-35-1
PDF: 978-1-950073-36-8
ePub: 978-1-950073-37-5
Kindle: 978-1-950073-38-2

Printed in the United States of America

GoToPublish
1-888-337-1724
www.GoToPublish.com
order@gotopublish.com

Our public lands–whether a national park or monument, wildlife refuge, forest, or prairie–make each one of us land-rich. It is our inheritance as citizens of a country called America.
Terry Tempest Williams "The Hour of Land"

COVER: Mount Grinnell

THIS PAGE: Wilbur Falls

Both in Glacier National Park, Montana

THE GREAT CENTENNIAL

Dedicated to the memory of my father in God's Word Dr. Victor Paul Wierwille, my parents Dr. and Mrs. Malcolm S. MacLean, Jr., and my Centennial folk heroes John Muir, John Denver, Stuart and Morris Udall, Theodore and Franklin Roosevelt, Stephen Mather, John D. Rockefeller, Jr., Timothy Treadwell, Henry David Thoreau, and Adolf and Marty Murie

To my immediate family, sister and brother-in-law Sandy and Luigi Manca, niece and nephew-in-law Nora and Neil Wickman, and great-niece Eowyn Wickman

Text and Photography by Les MacLean

<u>Top</u>: Bighorn Sheep and Prince of Wales Hotel   <u>Bottom</u>: Bighorn Ram on the Highline Trail   Waterton-Glacier International Peace Park

TABLE OF CONTENTS

Theme Song

National Parks:
God's Blessing and
America's Cornerstone

Page 61

Acknowledgements..................Next Page	Moose Wilbur....................................16
THE GREAT CENTENNIAL..................1	John Muir's Beauty as Well as Bread......17
THE HUNDRED YEAR CELEBRATION......3	A GREAT RIVER'S BEGINNING..............18
National Parks: God's Blessing and	GLACIER DYNASTY............................23
America's Cornerstone........................5	Song of The Mountains......................25
Montana:	The Glowing-robed King....................26
The Treasures of The Treasure State......6	Wilderness Monarch:
Glacier in My Heart............................7	Palace of The Grizzly........................28
Mountain Park Family........................8	Frontier North Fork:
Of Prairies and Pines.........................9	Home of Grizwold Grizzly..................32
Blue Ridge Beckoning......................10	The Good Old Days of Glaciers...........34
Memorial Dedication	Glacier Beyond The Pathway.............36
Stuart Udall and Edward Abbey..........11	HOME OF A PRESIDENT'S LEGACY
Castles in The Heavens....................12	Theodore Roosevelt National Park........44
The Great Chasm Drama..................13	THE WAPITI SONG
The Life and Times	Music of The Greater Yellowstone........51
of George Bird Grinnell....................14	THE NEXT HUNDRED YEARS
	AND BEYOND................................56

Mount Wilbur at Dawn   Glacier National Park

Left: Cades Cove Homestead Great Smoky Mountains National Park Right: Author in sweatshirt, a gift from Ron Cadrette, General Manager of Glacier Park, Inc.

ACKNOWLEDGEMENTS

Photography by Sandy Manca, author's sister

I wish to thank all the resources, and people, without whose information, and assistance, this book would not be possible. First, and foremost, I wish to thank God for the beauty of His unspoiled creation and my opportunities to enjoy, and conserve, in my writings and photography, for others to enjoy, His creation. The National Park Service must definitely be accredited for the wildlands they steward and the information I received both online and from many of her rangers, naturalists, volunteers, and store clerks. I wish to thank all my online information sources. The Ken Burns miniseries "National Parks, America's Best Idea" has been a wonderful source of both information and inspiration. Also a great source of inspiration, information, and famous quotes is conservation author Terry Tempest Williams especially from her book "The Hour of Land". The DVD "Theodore Roosevelt National Park Refuge of The American Spirit" is both a great information source and source of famous quotes from Terry Tempest Williams and our 26th President Theodore Roosevelt. I wish to accredit three state parks for their information and inspiration: West Virginia's Cacapon State Park (Cacapon the Shawnee name for "Medicine Waters") where I first fell in love with nature as a small boy, and revisited just a few years ago, South Dakota's Custer State Park for being my initial inspiration for the song "Of Prairies and Pines", and Montana's Missouri Headwaters State Park and National Historic Landmark. I wish to thank both employees, and management, of my former employer, Glacier Park, Inc., for having the privilege of working for them, allowing me to perform my Great Centennial program, for their sources of information, and their friendship; especially Vice President and General Manager Ron Cadrette and Glacier Park Lodge Manager Kathy Eiland. In the above photo of me riding on a Chicago CTA train, I am wearing the sweatshirt Ron gave me after my Great Centennial Celebration at Glacier Park Lodge. Last, but certainly not least, I wish to thank the Naperville Public Library (Naperville, Illinois) for the use of their computers, binders, and printers, their countless sources of information, and the lifesaving assistance of their dedicated employees especially the following lovely ladies Sweet Madison, Sweet Aqsa, Sweet Sarah, and a lovely young China doll, Sweet Weili.

Jones Columbine on Lee Ridge
Glacier National Park

THE GREAT CENTENNIAL

Above: Two bighorn rams sparring for dominance   Below right: The same rams after the fight; loser left, winner right

The Great Centennial, a time of discovery and rediscovery. A time of leaving behind a civilized life; the stress and pettiness of urban crowds, neighbor cheating neighbor, and all its lies and hypocrisy; to a life back in time, a time of great beauty, simplicity, sweet harmony, and unity, with man and beast alike.

Here-in I walked in the footsteps of Native American Nations, alongside the two great chiefs, the grizzly and gray wolf, in the subsistence pursuit of great buffalo herds; of Lewis and Clark, and their core of discovery, along the headwaters of the river of frontier history and culture, the great Missouri; and rediscovered the timeless, pristine wilderness of landmark conservationists George Bird Grinnell and Theodore Roosevelt.

A land where luminous grizzlies still hunt and forage in the shadow of white-threaded cathedral skylines, where soft-lit painted badlands still shelter great bison herds and free-roaming wild horses, and where massive prairie dog towns, covering a wild grassland sea, give refuge and sustenance to buffalo, antelope, elk, and deer. Here I rediscovered myself, and my fellow woman and man, in a brotherhood found only in the wild and pristine. It is a love, and heart sharing, amidst the edge of wild prairies and badlands, meandering untamed rivers, and mountain skylines gracing Heaven itself.

"..where massive prairie dog towns, covering a wild grassland sea, give refuge and sustenance to buffalo, antelope, elk, and deer."

<u>Above:</u> Black-tailed prairie dog and bison herd   Theodore Roosevelt National Park
<u>Below Left and right:</u> Grizzly bears and Lake Sherburne   <u>Below Middle:</u> Going-to-The-Sun Mountain   Glacier National Park

In the Great Centennial, my physical, and spiritual, self was renewed, in a time and place where our first national park, Yellowstone, and our first protected area, Yosemite, began a legacy going beyond national parks to state parks, forest preserves, wild rivers, and designated wilderness where we can escape to, and be blessed with great healing and tranquility.

"Where luminous grizzlies still hunt and forage in the shadow of white-threaded cathedral skylines..."

> Our national parks are not only our best idea but our highest ideal.
> I think that every time we walk into a national park, we make vows.
> We make vows that we will live beyond ourselves. We make vows
> that we will not just care about short-term gains but long-term vistas.
> Terry Tempest Williams

The Hundred Year Celebration

August 25, 1916 –
August 25, 2016

On August 25, 1916, thanks to the tireless work of Stephen Mather and Horace Albright, an agency was finally established for the administration, and stewardship, of our national parks, monuments, historic sites, and preserves, for the dual purpose of sanctuary for the people and preserving our great natural, and historical, wonders for future generations, and as quoted at the entrance of every national park, "For the benefit and enjoyment of the people". At the historic Glacier Park Lodge, built in 1913 by Glacier Park Company,, subsidiary of The Great Northern Railway, I would be lodged on the nights of August 24th and 25th, 2016, part of a two week celebration of the National Park Service Centennial. Because Hugh Grinnell, cousin of famed conservation journalist George Bird Grinnell, would be doing a program on the 25th, my program was scheduled for the 24th. On the eve of The Great Centennial, dressed in a fringed buckskin shirt and raccoon hat, with guitar in hand, I sang songs that I wrote about America's great wildlands, primarily the national parks. It would be at the lobby's stone fireplace and a time of song, and celebration, for one and all!

On the following pages are the songs that I played in front of a lit fireplace and before people of many ages

In celebration of the stewardship of our national parks, the following song is about the natural and human history of these great refuges of beauty and majesty. The song also incorporates my own parkland evolution and is a tribute, in thankfulness for their preservation and care, to the rangers, staff, and volunteers. It also commemorates authors, writers, business executives, news editors, and such stars of the political stage as Theodore and Franklin Roosevelt. To them, as well as to you who sit before me, this is your song.

NATIONAL PARKS
GOD'S BLESSING AND AMERICA'S CORNERSTONE

Written by Les MacLean in dedication to past and present heroes of our national parks

In Glacier, I witnessed a scene back in time, a grizzly family walked with royalty,
A pronghorn buck stood amidst the spires of the Badlands, a Teton moose was framed by a pine tree.
Atop a mountain, I gazed upon giant cathedrals, commanding vistas were filled with ice and snow,
I thanked God and country for our national parks where vast blue ribbon waters still flow.
Heavenly skylines of white-threaded mountains, misty shore-lines by a wave-strewn sea,
Gray wolves, grizzlies, and great buffalo herds, and icons of American history.
Arizona's Great Chasm carved by the Colorado, singing elk by thermals in Yellowstone,
My praise and thankfulness for the national parks, God's blessing and America's cornerstone.
The parkland was born in 1872 where geysers and grizzlies make their home,
Then came Muir's Yosemite, Mills' Rocky Mountain, and the Badlands where buffalo still roam.
Mather and Albright gave these lands cohesiveness as real protection came to our parklands,
Then the parks spanned from Main's Acadia to Alaska to the Channel Islands.
Wolf re-introductions, vast, wild Alaska, battlefields, and Indian cliff homes,
Parklands have gone beyond America's boundaries to where elephants and cheetahs still roam.
Heavenly skylines of white-threaded mountains, misty shorelines by a wave-strewn sea,
Gray wolves, grizzlies, and great buffalo herds, and icons of American history.
Arizona's Great Chasm carved by the Colorado, singing elk by thermals in Yellowstone,
My praise and thankfulness for the national parks, God's blessing and America's cornerstone.
As the bull elk sings to charm his hinds, the bighorn stands upon the edge of space,
I thank God for men like Grinnell and two Roosevelts for preserving this wild time and place.
Roaming this land of desert castle-rocks, frosty cascades, and the high Denali,
Though breathless, I'm thankful, for lands of majesty, where I am truly in the land of the free.
Heavenly skylines of white-threaded mountains, misty shore-lines by a wave-strewn sea,
Gray wolves, grizzlies, and great buffalo herds, and icons of American history.
Arizona's Great Chasm carved by the Colorado, singing elk by thermals in Yellowstone,
My praise and thankfulness for the national parks,
God's blessing and America's cornerstone.

CELEBRATING 100 YEARS OF THE NATIONAL PARK SERVICE
August 25, 1916 - August 25, 2016

When you hear the word "treasure", what do you think of? "Something that's special" said a tall GPI lady. It could mean   money, diamonds, rubies.... "something that's very important to you. It could be anything," said that same lady. That's right! Montana is known as the treasure state, not because of copper mining, or even tourism, but the God-given treasures that you are here to see, the treasures of the treasure state."

MONTANA
THE TREASURES OF THE TREASURE STATE

For great treasures people pan a mountain river or dig through the Comstock for gems of silver,

Or climb up the ladder of the great corporation,

Treasures for me are not gold nor money but the unspoiled gems of Big Sky Country

The pristine-ness of God's grand creation.

In the historic lore of a western ghost town, refreshing song of a tumbling cascade,

the majestic great bear on the mountainside, antelope band on the rolling prairie,

These rubies and gems of wild Montana are the treasures of The Treasure State.

Not gold but the bright golden rolling prairie, not silver but silver rivers and purple mountains,

To her beasts, blossoms, people I must truly elate,

To her grizzlies, goats, cascades, true gems of Montana, the treasures of The Treasure State.

From white-threaded skylines of God's Glacier Country to where the Jefferson, Gallatin, Madison form the wide Missouri, the purple– pink blossoms of the fairy slipper orchid, the humped silhouette of the grand grizzly bear,

and the bright golden aspens where the singing bull elk sounds.

Until the Lord returns and I'm headed home , it's the closest to Heaven for me,

Bitterroot Mountains, the white goat, and the great Yellowstone,

Wildness beyond what the eye can see.

Not gold but the bright golden rolling prairie, not silver but silver rivers and purple mountains,

To her beasts, blossoms, people I must truly elate,

To her grizzlies, goats, cascades, true gems of Montana, the treasures of The Treasure State

Lyrics and Photography by Les MacLean

Though I have been as far north as Alaska, as far south as Florida and Mexico, and have seen wildlife ranging from grizzly bears, wild horses, and caribou to badgers, prairie dogs, and barred owls; what famed conservationist George Bird Grinnell called "The Crown of The Continent" will always be my home in the mountains. In the alpenglow of its shimmering peaks, its colorful lady slipper orchids, its soaring eagles, and its timeless wilderness, there will always be Glacier in my heart.

GLACIER IN MY HEART

Lyrics and Photography by Les MacLean

Maroon bells of heather on Christmas tree leaves adorn tundra and springs along the Highline,
Pink laurels, sky pilot, and Jones columbine grace horns and arêtes
of the heavenly skyline.
In the soft light of dawn, in a meadow of red, glows the silver robe of a monarch grizzly,
On the edge of space walks the mighty bighorn as water cascades from the peaks to the sea.
Purple cathedrals and white-threaded skylines
From the depths of my soul will not part,
The frosty cascade, the white goat, the grizzly
Lord, I have Glacier in my heart.
Pink slipper blossoms along forest paths, rock amphitheaters with glacier blue,
A mountain goat feeds in snow lily gardens and Saint Nick's matterhorn stands proud and true.
Purple cathedrals and white-threaded skylines
From the depths of my soul will not part,
The frosty cascade, the white goat, the grizzly,
Lord, I have Glacier in my heart.
"In my heart and soul is the Glacier dynasty and a Glacier Park sister's embrace,
Throughout my life's journey, my heart will be in Glacier, the flowers, Glacierstock, and Chief
Mountain's grand face."
Purple cathedrals and white-threaded skylines
From the depths of my soul will not part,
The frosty cascade, the white goat, the grizzly,
Lord, I have Glacier in my heart.

One great blessing of the national parks, in my life, has been the privilege of working there. Especially in my nine summer seasons here in Glacier, both at Glacier Park Lodge and the Many Glacier Hotel. We were not only fellow workers but family. We worked together, shared hearts and wilderness trails, and cried in each other's arms at season's end. I just talked to the lovely cashier at "Country Market Mercantile" and she told me that fellow employees are still the loving, close-knit family of whom I had the privilege of working with back in the 1990s. Out here in the sticks, all we have are each other. Amidst the tranquil beauty of God's Glacier Country; just as it was when Glacier Park Lodge opened in 1913, when I worked here back in the 1990s, and today, August 24, 2016, on the eve of the National Park Service Centennial, we're still a mountain park family.

MOUNTAIN PARK FAMILY

Lyrics by Les MacLean and Photography by Les MacLean, Julia Kelso, Mike Bagby, and Julie Parks

My sister the naturalist, my brother the bellman, my uncle the dish dog,
my aunt the loyal lodge nurse, together we labor as a wilderness family united in song and in verse.
As brethren we travel through a white-threaded heaven watching white goats up high on a ledge,
a grizzly named Grizwold, a bighorn named Benny, live high on the vast meadow's edge.
We're a mountain park family with a kindred spirit united in a wilderness serene,
as brethren we labor, together we journey, our lives renewed in mountains pristine.
My sister the waitress, my brother the first cook, my cousins who clean rooms and tend bars,
at karaoke we sing, down rivers we raft, and ridge park roads in tour buses and cars.
With the maid I watched grizzlies, with the desk clerk I rode steeds,
the hotel nurse healed my heart and patched my knees,
as a family we hiked through aspens of gold and heard singing bull elk in the breeze.
We're a mountain park family with a kindred spirit united in a wilderness serene,
as brethren we labor, together we journey,
our lives renewed in mountains pristine.
As I journey through life, I will always be touched
by the memories of this wilderness home,
the forests, the flowers, but most of all this family
will be with me wherever I roam.
We're a mountain park family with a kindred spirit
united in a wilderness serene,
as brethren we labor, together we journey,
our lives renewed in mountains pristine.
We're a family in mountains pristine!

you came here from the east, you may have seen what I am going to sing about. In such pristine prairie-lands as Badlands, Windcave, and Theodore Roosevelt National Parks, the buffalo still roam, and the deer and the antelope still play in the land of prairies and pines.

OF PRAIRIES AND PINES

Lyrics and Photography by Les MacLean

The prairie comes to life with the song of a meadowlark and the barks of a prairie dog town, a noble antelope buck is on the wings of the wind in enchanted land where salsify is found. From Mount Harney's summit above the pines of the Black Hills to colorful spires of badlands, cottonwood-strewn rivers grace wild box canyons in the haven of Custer's last stand.

Where colorful rocks form castles in the skyline and in the wind a sea of wild grasses sway, I dream of prairies and pines where the buffalo still roam and the deer and the antelope still play.

Woolly giants all around me as bison roam free and in the sky, a red-tail on the wing, a tall ponderosa, a small golden rod, and a meadow where bluebirds still sing. It's hard to believe it's the new millennium on these plains which time left behind, through the eyes of Lewis, of Clark, and of Kelsey, I see the works of the Artist Divine.

Where colorful rocks form castles in the skyline and in the wind a sea of wild grasses sway, I dream of prairies and pines where the buffalo still roam and the deer and the antelope still play.

My lifelong wilderness quest began, as a small boy, in a West Virginia state park called Cacapon,, Shawnee for "the land of medicine waters". This was where I saw my first deer, hiked my first trail, and crossed my first stream. After a lifetime of wilderness exploration; from Alaska to Florida to Mexico to Canada, from the high Denali to the white sand dunes of the Florida panhandle; I returned to Cacapon, and her big sister, Shenandoah, Iroquois' for "the daughter of the stars", and answered the Blue Ridge Beckoning.

BLUE RIDGE BECKONING

A whippoorwill sings in the night-time forest where the medicine waters still flow,
a barred owl stares back from a branch above a brook where the daughter of the stars is aglow.
I see floral fireworks on shrubs of mountain laurel in the wild primeval of my heart,
the enrichment of the cascade, and the city of white-tails, from the depths of my soul will not part.
In the clouds that drape a blue mountain skyline, spotted fawn and mother beneath a lone tree,
pink azaleas that brighten shrub after shrub, I hear the call of the Blue Ridge beckoning me.
Shenandoah, Cacapon, Skyline Drive, New River Gorge, retreats of Appalachian lore,
a marmot singing over a greenstone cliff, a wild turkey standing on the forest floor.
A standing bear casts a shadow amidst the trees and ferns, a deer licks the salt on Skyline Drive,
a bright colored lizard in an outcrop's mini-canyon, they all make the Blue Ridge come alive.
In the clouds that drape a blue mountain skyline, spotted fawn and mother beneath a lone tree,
pink azaleas that brighten shrub after shrub,
I hear the call of the Blue Ridge beckoning me.
From a small boy who stares at his first running deer to a man who has almost seen it all,
both are enraptured by the misty fern meadow and the white stone crested waterfall.
In the clouds that drape a blue mountain skyline,
spotted fawn and mother beneath a lone tree,
pink azaleas that brighten shrub after shrub,
I hear the call of the Blue Ridge beckoning me.

Lyrics and Photography by Les MacLean

In case you don't know who are the small boy staring at his first running deer, and the man who has almost seen it all, they're both me.

In dedication to the memory of Edward Abbey, author of "Desert Solitaire", and Stuart Udall, author of "The Quiet Crisis" and Secretary of Interior during the administrations of Presidents John F. Kennedy and Lyndon B. Johnson, is a song about a colorful land of castle rocks, arches, and hoodoos, dear to both their hearts and mine, the land of Castles in The Heavens.

Monument Basin Canyonlands National Park

CASTLES IN THE HEAVENS

Lyrics and Photography by Les MacLean

The red Colorado meanders wild and free through a land of buttes and mesas as wide as the sea,
Prairie dogs chirp, eagles dance through the air, on slick rock bighorn dance through Abbey's solitaire.
Dawn paints orange light on barren bluffs and spires while blue clouds on the horizon come ablaze with orange fire,
The sweet smell of sage and a cool spring breeze, white sandstone rocks graced with pinion pine trees.
Castles in the heavens, islands in the sky, bright orange spires catch the eagle's eye,
Ed Abbey said it best of this rock desert sea, "life and love flowers best in the open and free".
The sandstone where I walk speaks of ancient history, of desert dunes and jungles and a vast inland sea,
Where the t-rex tromped through forests with a pride that wouldn't cease,
I sit before creation in tranquility and peace.
A meadowlark's music plays on clean desert air, I ponder my journey through Abbey's solitaire,
A golden arch frames buttes and mesas on high, castles in the heavens, islands in the sky.
Castles in the heavens, islands in the sky, bright orange spires catch the eagle's eye,
Ed Abbey said best of this rock desert sea, "life and love flowers best in the open and free".

Dedicated to the memory of Edward Abbey Naturalist and Author of Desert Solitaire

One of earth's seven great natural wonders, as well as one of America's great national parks, is a canyon of great beauty and vastness. Theodore Roosevelt, our nation's 26th president, said, of this canyon, " Leave this great wonder as it now is. The ages have been at work on it, and man can only mar it". This canyon has been a very integral part of my life, a great wonder that I call The Great Chasm Drama.

THE GREAT CHASM DRAMA

Lyrics and Photography by Les MacLean

Through the eyes of desert bighorn I gaze upon a wonder, a canyon deep and wide as the sea,
Where clouds drape cliffs that have the colors of the rainbow and soaring eagles and singing coyotes roam free.
The shining silver ribbon of the mighty Colorado made this canyon and carved out each cliff and butte,
To the music of the wind, I sing songs with the birds and to God and the river I salute.
Bobcat-eared squirrels eat tasty pinion nuts, cacti spread out like days of old,
A mile-deep labyrinth of mesas shine bright, in the Great Chasm Drama, God's creation unfolds.
A gun-toting marshal, a girl selling dime cokes, country singers on steam engine 29,
Through ponderosa and sage, where great elk herds wander, train passengers take a ride back in time.
In fall and winter '92, I lived and worked at this great wonder and witnessed a violent deer fight,
In the soft light of dawn, a chasm drama unfolds with gorges and cathedrals shimmering bright.
Bobcat-eared squirrels eat tasty pinion nuts, cacti spread out like days of old,
A mile-deep labyrinth of mesas shine bright, in the Great Chasm Drama, God's creation unfolds.

The program's grand finale was a sing-along of "National Parks: God's Blessing and America's Cornerstone".

Singleshot Mountain, where George Bird Grinnell killed a bighorn ram with a single shot before Glacier's park designation. The smaller photo is of Hugh Grinnell.

The Life and Times of George Bird Grinnell

On the evening of August 25, 2016, Hugh Grinnell, with his distant cousin's white moustache and dressed in the same kind of outdoor clothing, conducted and narrated a slide program, and talk, of one of the most famous conservationists in our nation's history. George Bird Grinnell was born September 20, 1849 in Brooklyn, New York. He received both his BA, in 1870, and PhD, in 1880, in Osteology. Beginning in 1870, he went on expeditions, out west, which included the Black Hills, led by General George Armstrong Custer, and, in 1875, in the capacity of a naturalist, he accompanied Colonel William Ludlow into Yellowstone. He began seeing the demise of many wildlife species, especially bison and elk, because there were no laws protecting them. He also became interested in the cultures, and welfare, of Native Americans. From 1890 until 1911, he was the senior editor, and publisher, of "Forest and Stream" magazine. He used this capacity for sustained campaigns against market hunting and for game laws to regulate hunting in all states. He initiated an investigation into poaching in Yellowstone. The resulting exposure of the poaching activity led to the passing of the Yellowstone Park Protection Act in 1894, a keystone to national park legislation. In the summer of 1885, he explored the part of Montana which would become Glacier National Park on May 11,1910. a large part of, what was behind Glacier becoming a national park, were his writings of the "Crown of The Continent". He was as much the reason we have Glacier as John Muir was for Yosemite and Enos Mills was for Colorado's Rocky Mountain National Park. In his early life, he lived on the Manhattan estate of naturalist John J. Audubon, where he would see bald eagles and the sky often blackened with the, now extinct, passenger pigeon. In 1886, he founded the National Audubon Society and served as its director for 26 years. Along with fellow sportsman, and conservationist, Theodore Roosevelt, he cofounded the Boone and Crockett Cub in 1887, and was its president from 1910 to 1927.

He was a landmark conservationist as well as a naturalist, journalist, author, and scientist. Though blessed with a lovely wife, half his age, he had no children. Nevertheless, any Grinnell in the United States is related to him, including Hugh. He became part of the ages on April 11, 1938, at the age of 88, having lived a long and full life. Many of Glacier's features are named after him: Grinnell Glacier, Upper Grinnell Lake, Grinnell Lake, Grinnell Falls, the red-colored geological formation Grinnell Argillite, and the peak, in the alpenglow photo on this book's front cover, Mount Grinnell. Fishercap Lake is so named from Grinnell's Blackfeet name.

" Many, O Lord, my God, are thy wonderful works which thou hast done, and thy thoughts to us-ward, they cannot be reckoned up in order unto thee: if I would declare and speak of them, they are more than can be numbered".

Psalm 40:5

The lofty skyline in a luminous alpenglow, the lordly grizzly glowing like a halo in a mountain meadow, the buffalo herd thundering across the prairie, coneflower and goldenrod dancing with prairie wind, a few, among many, of the wonderful works the Lord, my God, hast done. The white goat dancing, at heavenly heights, on a cliff, the mighty ram, in a full-curled crown, silhouetted on the misty Highline, red stripes, on white spires, at the edge of the prairie, and beavers, luminated on a glowing river, in dawn's early light; if I would declare and speak of them, they are more than can be numbered. One more of God's wonderful works, I would see on the morning of August 27, 2016, would be a young bull moose, named "Wilbur", having breakfast in a lovely mountain lake. While hiking the Swiftcurrent Pass trail, through a dense conifer forest above Fishercap Lake, a woman, with her husband, coming back up from the lake, told me that there was a moose down at the lake. Immediately I hiked down to the lake in anticipation of a symbolic wilderness scene. Sure enough, at the lake's west end, was a young, small antlered bull moose with a blackish brown coat and a light brown shoulder hump, eating water plants.

To the far right, Moose Wilbur's fan base, his silhouette near the lake shore directly beneath Mount Wilbur and Bullhead Point

The lake was a combination of dark green, and turquoise blue, with its shorelines graced with the conical blue-green canopies of subalpine fir. All this was in the shadow of the lofty gray and buff arêtes of Swiftcurrent Mountain, Mount Wilbur, and Bullhead Point. The sky was soft lit with white clouds and patches of light blue. The prominent peak was Mount Wilbur so I decided to give our ungainly, ungulate friend the name "Moose Wilbur". It was like a scene in a wilderness adventure movie and time stood still. Even the smallest signs of civilization seemed to be in another time zone, and even on another planet! There were other observers, besides me, even closer to the moose than I, but he kept on dipping his head underwater, and emerging with more plants in his mouth, as a cascade of water poured from his neck and snout. He continued feeding, and focusing on his meal, as though we weren't even there. I snapped photo, after photo, taking full profiles, close-ups, combinations of moose and landscape, and, meanwhile, he actually moved closer to the other photographers and me. His damp coat glistened in the morning sun and his eyes gleamed like Christmas lights. As I continued taking photos, his fan base grew with people of all ages and backgrounds and cameras ranging from smart phones, and small Panasonics, to the big names like Canon and Nikon. After taking several photos with my big zoom lens, I switched to my smaller 28-80 zoom and took compositions like the photo above. After a while I left to continue my hike, thankful, not only for the photographic blessing of which Moose Wilbur was, but that despite people approaching him too close, he did not charge, nor even seem to get annoyed, and kept on feeding.

Top: Running Eagle Falls Glacier National Park   Bottom: Bull Moose Grand Teton National Park

Everybody needs beauty as well as bread, places to pray and play in, where nature may heal and cheer and give strength to body and soul alike. This natural beauty hunger is made manifest in our magnificent national parks.

John Muir

Images of The Confluence with beavers at dawn, at sunset, and at sunrise

A GREAT RIVER'S BEGINNING

Our great river of the frontier, the Missouri, begins her 2,341 mile journey, through seven states flowing into the Mississippi near Saint Louis, Missouri. It begins where the above beaver family is swimming and feeding, the confluence (known as the Confluence) of the Madison, and Jefferson, rivers in southwestern Montana's Missouri Headwaters State Park and National Historic Landmark. Roughly a mile downstream, the Gallatin flows in completing the formation of one of our nation's most famous rivers. The river was a major travel route of the famed Lewis and Clark, Core of Discovery, expedition, which arrived at these headwaters some time in late July, 1805, most likely being the first non-native Americans in the Three Forks Area. They named the three rivers Jefferson, Madison, and Gallatin. It was once a resource-rich hunting ground of such nations as the Blackfeet, Crow, Salish, and Shoshone. The Headwaters was the childhood home of the Core of Discovery's Shoshone guide, Sacagawea, before she was captured as a young girl. Then came fur trappers, settlers, and the frontier agricultural, and mining town of Gallatin City. Today, all that remains of this once booming 1860s town, are the skeletal remains of a once busy hotel and community center. Still, history continues, that of wise stewardship where rangers, artists, and authors have replaced fur trappers, cattlemen, and merchants. Here begins a river behind the growth of one nation under God.

The Gallatin River where it flows in, the final formation of the wide Missouri

Close-up of the beaver in the bottom photo

The Confluence of the Jefferson and Madison at Dawn

The hotel was not only an inn to weary travelers but the town's social center comparable to churches, and community centers, in today's small towns. Built by Jarvis Akin, it was once a bigger hotel until it closed its doors and sections were torn down and carted away elsewhere. I could still hear, in the back of my mind, voices of inn guests and towns' people along with the playing of a piano, what you hear in saloons of old west movies and TV progra*ms*.

Here begins a river behind the growth of one nation under God

Seeing that beaver family, right on the point of the Confluence, was truly a blessing from God, above what I could ask or think. I was thankful, not only for the timeless, living beauty brought to life by these wildland engineers, but for the advent of silk, and a change in the whim of fashion which saved the beaver from extinction. In the pre-Civil War days of the mountain man, beavers were worth their weight in gold as hats, and other beaver-made clothing, a bigger fad than the bell-bottom trousers, tidied t-shirts, and long hair of the late sixties and early seventies. Beavers were trapped, wherever they were found, long before the advent of game laws and conservation. Every time I see a beaver in the wild, I thank God for silk and a change in fashion. Today, beavers are wide-spread and quite beneficial as their dams make ponds, and lakes, lifelines not only for fish such as brook trout; and their predators such as the osprey, bald eagle, and man; but for ungulates such as moose, and elk, providing forage that grows in, and around, these ponds and lakes. I have even been blessed with photographing beavers back in my home state of Illinois!

Even though Missouri Headwaters is not a national park, this is a region of discovery, and frontier history, that led to the birth of our national parks, wilderness, and our conservation heritage. Though administered by a Montana state agency, it is a national historic landmark with abundant flora, and fauna, little changed from the days of the Native American nations, home of such wildlife as, not only beavers, but golden and bald eagles, osprey, and white-tailed and mule deer. As I witnessed the sun setting on this great river frontier, I thought of what famed singer-songwriter John Denver said about looking forward to a brand new tomorrow; one of hope and new beginnings.

GLACIER DYNASTY

In the majestic northern Rockies, a Glacier Dynasty rules supreme

Swiftcurrent Glacier, Swiftcurrent Mountain, and the Swiftcurrent Pass Trail photographed September 2006

In August 2016, only snow patches were left of the glacier

From sea and sediment, mountains arose.

Glacial ice was the Divine Sculptor's blade carving out lofty peaks and deep valleys

Then these lofty peaks, and deep valleys came to life; first with forests, meadows, prairie, and alpine gardens followed by fauna, great and small, from the grizzly, the bighorn, the mountain goat, and the moose to the wolverine, the pine marten, the frosty marmot, and the vole. The Glacier Dynasty was born and on May 11, 1910, when man gave this Dynasty great recognition as a national park. On June 18, 1932, our brotherhood, with Canada, was confirmed as Alberta, Canada's Waterton Lakes National Park, and Glacier National Park, were united as Waterton-Glacier International Peace Park. In 1995, Glacier received global recognition as a world heritage site. On June 4, 1991, the Glacier Dynasty took me into her kingdom when I began working nine summer seasons working for Glacier Park, Inc. What became, and still is, a part of me is its majestic song of the mountains.

SONG OF THE MOUNTAINS
Lyrics and Photography by Les MacLean

Just like John Muir I've come to the mountains, to aspens, pines, firs I've come home,
Blue glacial ice, frosty cascades, and high cliffs where mountain goats roam.
King Grizzly silhouettes high on a slope, his robe glows beneath the sun,
In a full curl crown a ram posts sentinel, on an outcrop marmots have fun.
Song of the mountains echoes across the canyons,
rock and snow glow in the heavens above,
Montana's range of light shines throughout the skyline,
a portrait, a sculpture made with God's love.
Blue icebergs float on green alpine lakes, glacier lilies grace a mountain stream,
A meadow unfolds with paintbrush and phacelia, Lord, am I having a dream?
Father how manifold are your works that surround me, made with great wisdom and detail,
The awesome landscape sings a grand melody, through cathedrals wind starts to wail.
Song of the mountains echoes across the canyons,
rock and snow glow in the heavens above,
Montana's range of light shines throughout the skyline,
a portrait, a sculpture made with God's love.

THE GLOWING-ROBED KING

"On a mountainside, I stood in wonder, as to my present surprise,
walking upslope like a lordly emperor a frosty giant of mammoth size.
A wilderness ruler, he's so proud and sure, crowned with a blond bearded face,
with humped shoulders like a mountain he conquers the land as he gallops
with speed and with grace.

An awesome grizzly giant walks his rocky domain
as beneath the sun shines the Glowing-robed King,
all glory and praise to Divine-Artist God
as to his majesty the high mountains sing.

With massive muscles he floats across the tundra as he feeds on the lilies and the grass,
like a halo he glows silhouetted on a ridge as with ease a ascends the mountain pass.
I must be dreaming, or back in time, thank God for this answer to prayer,
with grace he walks on his lofty domain as our Father's mountain music fills the air.

An awesome grizzly giant walks his rocky domain
as beneath the sun shines the Glowing-robed King,
all glory and praise to Divine-Artist God
as to his majesty the high mountains sing.

On a sunny, late-June day, I was hiking along the Swiftcurrent Pass Trail, hiking the open terrain, amidst dwarfed aspen and fir, in the vicinity of the glistening, blue-green waters of Bullhead Lake. I looked off to my right, at the open, sloped terrain at the foot of the massive arête of Mount Wilbur. A distinctive brown dot, glistening in the sun's rays, caught my eye and I knew it was something alive. Hiking behind me were two young men, and when I looked through my telephoto lens, and saw a massive head, and muscular physique, I replied "grizzly!", in a sharp whisper, and the two hikers stopped in their tracks. One of the men was carrying a pair of binoculars and I asked if I could borrow them. He loaned them to me as I looked through them at, what looked like a 600 pound blondish-brown male, bigger than most grizzlies I've seen in Alaska. After giving the hiker's binoculars back to him, and thanking him, I left the trail in pursuit of a photographic trophy.

Was this for real? Was I dreaming or watching a movie like "The Bear", "Walking Thunder", or "Wilderness Family"? This frosty wilderness giant was just as real as the grasses beneath my feet and the mountains above my head! It was as though I were an 1800s Blackfeet Indian or a member of the Lewis and Clark expedition. This glowing-robed king, emperor of the mountains, walked in a lordly gait, and seemed to float across rock slabs, scree, and grassy slopes. I knew, right then and there, this was his home, his kingdom, and that I was no longer the dominant animal. I did pray, for the well-being of myself and the bear as well as successful photography. I had no fear but reasonable caution mixed with this "moment of truth" in wildlife photography. My approach was indirect as I paced myself through willow, aspen, and other shrubbery, crossed a streambed, and circled a clump of lodgepole pines. For the next few yards I could no longer see him because of the trees, and shrubs, in front of me. He could easily be concealed in the brush. To lessen the likelihood of a surprise encounter, my movements were slow and precise, and my eyes were ever scanning. I finally reached an open hillside and, from that vantage point, I saw the grizzly emerge from some pines, crossing a scree toward some rocks, eating glacier lilies and grasses as he went. I was now in camera range yet not too close for comfort. After reading Dr. Stephen Herero's book, "Bear Attacks: Their Causes and Avoidance", I took his advice in making my presence known to the bear to avoid surprising him. I yelled "hey bear!" a couple of times. He did look back then continued his walking and grazing, as I continued taking photos. Like a three-dimensional painting, there he was, climbing with gallantry, the same terrain where I fought slippery rocks, gravel, brush, and gravity for my forward progress. On my way back to the trailhead, two lady rangers, and many hikers, would know of my find. Back at the trailhead was that bright orange sign that had not been there when my hike began this morning: "Grizzly in area traversed by this trail, stay alert!" With massive head, mountain-high shoulders, and a huge muscular bulk, he walked in his high country palace. His frosty silhouette glowed like a halo; this wilderness ruler, mountain emperor, the Glowing-robed King.

WILDERNESS MONARCH
THE PALACE OF THE GRIZZLY

We are not protecting the grizzlies from extinction; they are protecting us from the extinction of experience as we engage in a world beyond ourselves. The very presence of a grizzly returns us to an ecology of awe. We tremble at what appears to be a dream yet stands before us on two legs and roars.

Terry Tempest Williams "The Hour of Land"

On September 26, 2006, in Montana's Glacier National Park, I was driving a road, not only taking me to the Many Glacier Hotel, and Swiftcurrent Motor Inn, but into a wilderness time left behind. The Many Glacier Valley was full of the brilliance of Autumn with aspens of gold and the scarlet and orange of maple, ash, and dogwood. Soaring, precipitous mountains formed high, protective walls sheltering a rugged landscape of conifers, aspens, singing streams, rock flats, and turquoise lakes, from the rest of the world. The vistas, and majestic mountain scenery, were never-ending, especially in soft lighting with the sun hiding behind high clouds. It looked more like a Rembrandt painting than a live scene, but alive it was. Along the road were signs that said "no parking, stopping, or standing". This was to give elbow room for bears, who were out, and about, feeding up for their winter sleep. As I approached the driveway to the Many Glacier Hotel, now closed for the season, parked vehicles were all about and people were out with cameras, binoculars, and spotting scopes, all facing upward toward Mount Altyn. I asked what they were looking at and one man told me there were grizzlies on the ridge behind me. Immediately, I parked my car and grabbed my already assembled camera, and tripod, with a 100-300 zoom lens attached to a 2x tele converter. I learned, long ago, especially in grizzly country, to always be camera ready. High on an outcrop of the skeletons of windblown whitebark pines, and small aspens, were two sub adult grizzly bears, quite likely brothers due to their large size.

When I looked through my camera's viewer, it was as though I were up on the outcrop with them! They had beautiful coats of frost-tinted gray and brown, and one of them had a distinctive shoulder hump like the hump on a camel's back. Though they grazed like cattle, they moved, like princes in a parade, across steep, and rocky, terrain. After climbing up, and over, the outcrop, they were soon out of sight. Moments later, they were following the gravel-bottom terrain of Swiftcurrent Creek so we headed for the road turnout overlooking the creek. Above us, a sow black bear, with two cubs, grazed near a clump of glowing small aspens. Even though we knew that we were sandwiched between two sets of bears, we remained there, awestruck by a truly wild, and wilderness drama, likened to an Alaskan wilderness accessible only by bush plane! Following silver waters, and surrounded by towering subalpine firs, and a slope adorned with the yellow, scarlet, red, and orange of autumn, frosty grizzly princes boldly walked through their wilderness palace. Moments later, they emerged from some aspens, along the rocky shores of Lake Sherburne. At that time, a ranger's squad car pulled up alongside us, and a lovely, brunette lady ranger stepped out and asked us to return to our vehicles, and leave. With the black bear family above us, and the grizzly siblings below us, she could see the danger we were in and she was also wanted the bears to have their space. As much as I hated to stop taking photos, I knew the importance of what the ranger told us. Back at camp, after a dinner of luncheon meat, peas, and diced tomatoes, covered with American cheese, I again used the propane stove to heat up dishwater to clean up the dishware and any spills made on the picnic table. Since a bear's sense of smell is seven times that of a bloodhound, I had to clean up even the smallest spill or stain. Since the regular bathrooms, with sinks, were closed for the season, I dumped the dishwater in one of the bear-proof garbage cans since dumping it on the ground, or in a pit toilet, would also attract bears. Afterwards, I walked through camp and met a lovely young lady, named Marianne (I have a cousin by that name!) who also saw the grizzlies earlier today. While we were talking about grizzlies, a snowshoe hare showed up behind her and I pointed it out to her. Though rabbits and hares are common place, a snowshoe hare is special, an icon like the grizzly and the bighorn. The name "snowshoe" comes from its very large feet used to travel over deep snow. Though the hare was still mostly brown, it was showing signs of transforming into winter white. Its feet were white along with white fringing around the ears. The changing color on the hare, bears covering vast landscapes to gain calories, and brilliant autumn colors, all told the same story. Winter was on its way!

The following day, I learned the true meaning of perfect timing after turning back from hiking roughly a mile upstream along Boulder Creek. Had I turned back sooner, or continued my journey, I would have missed the great blessing I am about to share with you. I passed the park's entrance station and the aspens opened up to Windy Creek Meadow. Several vehicles were parked on both sides of the road and people were out with cameras, and spotting scopes, facing where the meadow slopes down to Lake Sherburne. I looked down toward the lake and, sure enough, a large blondish silhouette with two blond fur balls following behind.

It could not have been anything but a sow grizzly bear and her first-year cubs floating through hay-colored, wind-blown grasses. Windy Creek Meadow definitely lived up to its name as a powerful wind made the grasses sway and the lake's light blue waters white-cap. I also had a tough time keeping my tripod-mounted camera steady and preventing a blur in the photos. Nevertheless, the wind did add action and drama to the scene, grizzlies in their domain, wild, natural, and dominant. I left the road and walked another 50 yards, or so, following this young couple. When I reached a small clump of aspens, I stopped, and so did the wife. The husband continued his approach until I told him to stop as he was getting too close to one of the most protective mothers in the animal kingdom. I was glad he heeded my warning as the last thing I wanted was to witness a bear mauling! For as long as the grizzlies were down by the lake, I continued photographing them until I ran out of film. I headed back to the car and reloaded my camera. By that time, the bears had left the beach and were headed up to the road.

Before the sow vanished into some aspens, I anticipated where she would re-emerge out onto the road and pointed my camera to that part of the road. The cubs were 50 yards behind her. Moments later, she emerged from the aspens and onto the road with single-mindedness knowing her cubs were following her. I managed to snap two photos of her crossing the road, one of the photos four pages back, before she vanished into the aspens just the other side of the road. I hoped to catch her cubs crossing the road, on film, but a ranger squad car pulled out between the cubs and me. The same lady ranger, of whom we saw, yesterday, asked us to get back in our cars, and we did. Before driving off, I stuck my upright fist out the car window and shouted "Grizzlies rule!" as a memorial tribute to crock hunter Steve Irwin who, sadly, was killed by a stingray only a week before my trip. The song, I wrote about the grizzly, is called "The Glowing-robed King". She was his glowing-robed queen. She, too, had humped shoulders like a mountain, was a conqueror of her domain, and, at times, the sun would outline the blondish silhouettes of her and her cubs. We, truly, were a privileged people, watching the very hallmark of North American wilderness, living noble and free in this wild and timeless land.

 # Frontier North Fork
Home of Grizwold Grizzly

Grizwold Grizzly

Grizwold Grizzly

Except for a narrow, winding, and pothole and washboard-ridden road, along the North Fork, in the northwest part of Glacier National Park, you would think you're back in the days of Lewis and Clark. Wolves returned to Glacier on their own, after being exterminated early in the 20th Century, in the 1980s, first seen on Camas Lake, the famed "Magic Pack". It is an area of diverse vegetation, and landscapes, ranging from dense cedar-hemlock rainforests to more open forests which include Montana's state tree, the ponderosa, Engelmann spruce, lodgepole pine, subalpine fir, and North America's deciduous conifer, the larch, also known as the "tamarack", blue-ribbon lakes and streams, and lush, marshy and dense grass meadows often teaming with elk and white-tailed deer. It is home to a diversity of wildlife which include wolves, pine martens, moose, elk, loons, bald eagles, and black and grizzly bears. This is where I met Grizwold Grizzly on July 22, 1992.

Livingston Range viewed from a meadow along Camas Creek

At the south end, the road began with a large sign warning us that the road was narrow, rough, and with blind corners and few turnouts. I was driving a small Mazda hatchback with the company of two Glacier Park, Inc., coworkers of mine, Rich and Amanda. The first part of the drive was through a wall of forest green, a dense and dark rainforest. In the old fable of "The Tortoise and the Hare", the moral is that slow and easy wins the race. I took it slow and easy to survive the race! I was especially glad to take it slow as, around one blind corner, was a deep rut, almost as big as my car. It was well worth driving this rough, and primitive, road to see Montana wilderness through the eyes of early explorers and the Native American nations. This especially held true when I looked upon the bubbling waters of Camas Creek and the virgin green of McGee and Christiansen Meadows. Forests slightly opened up and rainforest was gradually replaced by large, quaking aspens, many of them with trunks over a foot in diameter, and looking to be over 75 feet tall, along with ponderosa pine. Rich spotted one roadside aspen with black bear paw prints ascending its trunk. We passed one natural mineral lick that was graced with tall grasses, and resembling a large moon crater. A small band of white-tailed does, with beautiful, soft-lit, red coats, fed upon the minerals. While driving through a forest of large ponderosa pine, we found fresh bear scat on the road and slowed to a crawl. Seconds later, Rich pointed out a small, brown-colored black bear seeking a meal of leaves and berries. As we entered a large ravine, the forest floor became ripe with service, also known as Saskatoon, berries. Fresh, berry-ridden bear scat was in the middle of the road. Seconds later, Amanda pointed to a roadside log where two, large sibling bears, with long snouts, fed on berries just 15 feet to the left of the car. The bears had light brown coats with blond tips on their backs. I saw the bottom of one of their paws and each claw was as long as my index finger. Amanda pointed to the side profile and we noticed the distinctive shoulder hump. These were grizzlies!

North Fork Skyline in Autumn, featuring Rainbow Peak, the tallest in the photo

They looked to weigh at least 300 pounds, each, and not only did we see the grizzlies but heard them make chomping sounds, as they fed, along with heavy breathing, as plain as the sounds of the birds singing. One beautiful sight for me, in the photo two pages back, was a pink fireweed in front of the back part of one of the bear's side profile. Meet Grizwold Grizzly, the founding CEO of Grizwold Grizzly Publications! He, and his twin brother, Grison, looked handsome as their silhouettes glowed from sunrays shooting through the forest canopy. As we watched, and photographed, from inside the car, the bears were too busy feeding to show either fear or aggression. We would spend the rest of the day exploring more of the North Fork Valley as far as Bowman Lake. Though I have made many return trips to the North Fork being blessed with seeing white glacier lilies, pine martens, a loon at Trout Lake, a bald eagle at Camas Lake, and a split second sighting of a wolf in 1999, I most remember meeting my iconic wilderness commander, Grizwold Grizzly!

THE GOOD OLD DAYS OF GLACIERS

THE GOOD OLD DAYS OF GLACIERS

Previous Page at Bottom: Sperry Glacier and Mountain Goats
Sperry Glacier Ice Art   1994

This Page: Hikers on Grinnell Glacier 1991

In 1850, Glacier National Park had 150 glaciers. When I began my nine summer seasons, working for Glacier Park, Inc. in 1991, Glacier had 40 glaciers and we could hike on Grinnell Glacier as late as 1995. In September 2006, from the Swiftcurrent Pass trail by Bullhead Lake, I could see a full wedge-shaped Swiftcurrent Glacier on the side of Swiftcurrent Mountain. In August 2016, from the same viewpoint, only scattered white snow patches were left. In 2015, only 26 glaciers were left. It is predicted that within the next ten years, Glacier's namesake will be gone. With all this, along with all the forests I have seen torched in my recent Glacier visits, and a yellow algae called "rock snot" recently plaguing many of the stream bottoms, no one can tell me that climate change is not happening!

Piegan Glacier

1994

Weasel Collar Glacier
1997

In late July 1997, I took these photos during a hike back from Hole-in-The-Wall Campground

GLACIER BEYOND THE PATHWAY

Shangrila is accessible either by level 3 rock climbing after leaving the Swiftcurrent Pass trail or by following goat paths uphill from the southeast end of Iceberg Lake.

ROCKY MOUNTAIN SHANGRILA

Sitting on the peaceful shores of Rocky Mountain Shangrila, I am in total solitude yet not alone because the Father is with me. Unspoiled beauty surrounds me, is above me, before me, and at my feet. I am face to face with mountaintops and high hanging valleys. Meadows of grass, rock, and multicolored flower gardens, interspersed with stunted and matted firs and pines, surround me, as I am perched on the rock-strewn shores of a turquoise lake. Snow forms blankets over meadows, crests over the lake's waters, and fingers and dots over a glacier-carved, bowl-like mountain landscape. No road, no trails, nor any of man's intrusions reach Shangrila. It offers sanctuary to the soul for the few who choose the painstaking journey up the cliffs, scree, and goat paths, and through the maize and tangle of thick shrubs to enter this alpine Eden. It is the palace of the monarch grizzly who feeds on her grasses, glacier lilies, and ground squirrels as his golden, humped-shouldered silhouette glows beneath the sun. I sit with the mighty bighorn on a carpet of paintbrush and fireweed. This mountain gladiator, with powerful neck and shoulder muscles, massive curled horns, and feet which scale the greatest heights, rests before me with all the sureness of an Olympic champion. Mountain goats, in their luminous coats of white, float over the tundra above me. A multicolor assortment of wildflowers has made Shangrila a larger than life rock garden. On rock, and grassy tundra, are the bright reds of paintbrush and fireweed, the blue teacup-shaped blossoms of bog gentilian, and the tiny, purplish-blue blossoms of sky pilot and forget-me-nots.

Top: Shangrila
Left: Benny The Bighorn
Right: Glacier Lily, Globeflowers, and ferns
Previous Page: Kakitos Mountain viewed from White Calf Mountain

Amidst the meadow grasses, not lost in the floral assortment of species and colors, are the white and yellow of globeflowers, the bright yellow of glacier lilies, and the maroon red leaves of tiny ferns. Wildflowers also form a painter's palate of colors along huge boulders, the rocky course of Shangrila Creek, and where stone terraces are draped with cold, dancing waters that drain mountaintops. Alongside a cascading brook are the maroon bells of mountain heather atop Christmas tree leaves and the pink and yellow blossoms of monkeyflower. I am in another dimension, another earth, far above the lies, confusion, and pettiness of Satan's civilization. Here there are no jet planes knocking down skyscrapers, no politicians lying and stealing to win elections, no murders, no thefts, and no bad economies. Virgin beauty surrounds me and great peace and tranquility is from within. Exemplified, and amplified, here, is how the earth, and its fullness, is the Lord's, and how this loving Creator opens His hand and satisfies the desire of every living thing. In this alpine temple, I live and thrive, again, renewed in spirit, full of joy, and intimate in my fellowship with God while amidst His handiwork. Sitting on the peaceful shores of Rocky Mountain Shangrila, I am in total solitude yet not alone because the Father is with me.

Bighorn ewes traversing syncline cliff photographed from across upper reaches of Windy Creek

WINDY CREEK DRAINAGE AND UP AND OVER THE MOUNTAIN

If you hike the trail to Poia Lake, and Red Gap Pass, from the trailhead in the Many Glacier Valley, cross the footbridge over Windy Creek, and up to the top of the ravine, on the other side, well worn elk trails will take you upstream along Windy Creek to its source. The above photo was taken above the creek of this east facing cliff of folds called a syncline. Bighorn ewes were walking along these folds like you and I would hike a trail.

After taking this photo, I had lunch sitting on a red rock with wave ripples on top, a rock that was once at the bottom of a shallow inland sea, Grinnell argillite. A syncline is a folding of rock from compression as a part of mountain building. Younger layers are found closer to the center, becoming older as they move out. Windy Creek Drainage is prime habitat for, not only elk and deer, but marmots and grizzlies as I had often heard a loud whistle, from a hoary marmot, echo from the cliffs above, and found diggings, and huge boulders, requiring ten NFL linemen to lift, tossed aside like a soccer ball. On September 2, 1992, I hiked beyond the Windy Creek headwaters, and up Appikuni Ridge, following trails made by bighorn sheep and mountain goats, up a steep grade. Truly Windy Creek lived up to her name, that day, as I could barely hold my ground with powerful gusts which almost picked me up and carried me away. To keep from being blown to the ground, or into a rock, I had to keep bent knees, spread legs, and a low profile often bending my body forward to keep the wind from blowing me on my back. I was the only human being for as far as the eye could see! Even a minor injury could be life-threatening! The wind blew my hat away into the vastness!

Lady Stephanie Falls (Named by Author) on wooded bench above Kennedy Creek on the north side of Appikuni Mountain

When I stopped to rest, eat, and drink plenty of water, I looked up to see mountain goats wandering across the ridgetop. As I ascended, the ridge was higher up than it looked but as I climbed the view became more panoramic with a full spectrum of the canyon's white cliffs, alpine springs, scrub firs, and moss and lichen tundra. When I reached the mountaintop, what stood before me was vast, treeless tundra unfolded in orange blotches of lichen. It looked like a stretch of tundra in northern Alaska's Brooks Range. High, lofty cliffs, and crags, were a brilliant crimson red, part of the Grinnell Argillite formation. I saw no other human sign, not even a faded footprint and I felt like the first explorer on a remote mountaintop. The wind blew so hard that all I could hear was the wind putting pressure on both my face and eardrums. I swore that the wind would continue to howl through my ear canals long after it ceased blowing! My feet, and ankles, were also sore from a steep climb through loose scree. Still, the discomfort paled in comparison to both the solitude and eagle-eye vista of surrounding mountaintops spanning to 40-50 miles away, including the blue and white sentinel of Mount Merritt and the sun-glistened ice-mass of Old Sun Glacier. The gray and white cliff face of Waterton-Glacier's crown, Mount Cleveland(10,466 feet), stared back at me from beyond the top of Seward Mountain. After enjoying the view, I descended down the other side, a steep trek through unstable rocks and boulders. I made it to a bench above Kennedy Creek where, in a small meadow, there was a pond of cold, clear turquoise water, which had no incoming, nor outgoing streams. I took a closer look to see steep drop-offs from the shoreline into a hole that looked bottomless. Perhaps this pond was fed by an underground aquifer. Afterwards, I did some downhill bushwhacking through a spruce-fir forest.

Without warning, I found myself on a slippery, moss-covered cliff of limestone. There went my footing as I began to fall, heading toward the jagged rocks below. Uncertain whether or not I would grab a friendly fir or a spiny spruce, a branch of either one, was better choice than serious injury or death. Fortunately, I wound up grabbing friendly fir and, as I continued flying through the air, I continued grabbing conifer branches to break my fall. Then my backside slammed into the side of a small cliff. That did smart but I had nothing more than a few scrapes on my wrists, and hands. I continued my steep, downward trek, bushwhacking, and often ski-jumping as I continued grabbing tree branches to break my fall. Still, the bushwhacking was worth it as the forest, and its trees, and limestone formations were quite beautiful. The highlight was where a tributary brook tumbled over two small black and gray cliffs graced with mountain ash. The stones were terraced, adorned with moss, and the cascade looked like strands of frosty hair singing their way through the forest. It was one of the prettiest cascades I had ever seen and it stood out like a jewel in the primeval darkness. On the previous page is a photo of this waterfall, and years later, I would name it "Lady Stephanie Falls" after the sweet, and lovely, receptionist of a Naturopathist I used to patronize. I finally reached the floor of the canyon where I crossed Kennedy Creek and laced myself through willows and back on the trail where my hike began, except that I was now upstream from Poia Lake and downstream from Red Gap Pass. The remaining journey was a long return hike past Poia Lake, up and over Swiftcurrent Ridge, down to Swiftcurrent Ridge Lake, and back to the trailhead. Still it was a beautiful hike especially where I passed a large, roaring waterfall coming down from Yellow Mountain. Later on, I was startled by a large cow elk running through the forest as her pounding hooves were in rhythm with my beating heart. Before reaching the trailhead I heard the singing of a bull elk in a nearby meadow, the sound of music in autumn.

Bull moose high above Boulder Creek accessible by bushwhacking a forested ridge above Sherburne Dam or ascending open slopes just upstream from where Boulder Creek flows into Swiftcurrent Creek

OF PATHWAYS AND MOUNTAINTOPS

Two Glacier Park Inc. employees, 1996 hiking companions of mine, atop Dancing Woman Peak

Whether it's bushwhacking, following the paths of goats and grizzlies, or climbing to the top of one of Glacier's shining mountains, the true Glacier dynasty unfolds beyond any road or hiking trail. Scenic vistas are like looking out from a window in Heaven at larger-than-life cathedrals which shimmer like diamonds and pearls. It is where the grizzly is its glowing-robed king and massive-curled rams stand, with pride, on the edge of space. Wildflowers unfold in living color with all the colors of an artist's palate, in alpine gardens on mountaintops and massive high ridge tundra. Be it Rocky Mountain Shangrila, Boulder Creek, Windy Creek Drainage, or the summits of Dancing Woman, Henkel, or Cleveland, you enter a surreal garden where you can reach up and touch the hand of God.

In the majestic northern Rockies, a Glacier dynasty rules supreme!

Chief Mountain and healthy whitebark pines viewed from Lee Ridge

Moss Campion also on Dancing Woman's summit

HOME OF A PRESIDENT'S LEGACY
Theodore Roosevelt National Park

Wind Canyon and The Little Missouri River

"A place of inspiration, imagination, and transformation. It remains a refuge of the American spirit"
Terry Tempest Williams-Conservation Author

On Valentines Day, 1884, in the same New York home, Theodore Roosevelt lost his wife to childbirth complications and his mother to typhoid fever. After leaving his infant daughter in the care of nearby relatives, he returned to Dakota Territory where, in previous years, he hunted bison. He returned to these badlands seeking healing, comfort, and renewed spirit. Along the Little Missouri River, he purchased a ranch of which he named the Elkhorn Ranch. It was the time he spent here, in this pristine land of colorful spires and bluffs, abundant elk and bison, and vast prairie rich in wildflowers, grass, and countless prairie dog towns, where he had the initial inspiration for his famed conservation legacy. Because of the time he spent here, he became the greatest conservationist in presidential history. On April 25, 1947, Theodore Roosevelt National Memorial Park was signed into law by President Harry Truman. On November 10, 1978, President Jimmy Carter signed, into law, the bill establishing Theodore Roosevelt National Park. During my Great Centennial excursion I visited this 70,448-acre park as both my first, and last, major visit of an itinerary which also included Glacier National Park and Missouri Headwaters State Park and National Historic Landmark. The Little Missouri is the parkland's lifeblood flowing through prairies and canyons rich in colorful, and detailed, rock formations which include hoodoos and a petrified forest. Except for the absence of wolves and grizzlies, this prairie wilderness; and its grasslands, forests, and cottonwood-strewn river bottoms; still had the same buffalo, elk, antelope, and not only prairie dog towns, but vast prairie dog cities as when such great Native American nations, as the Lakota and Cheyenne, ruled the plains.

Badland rock formation whose stripes are made of iron oxide

An old west scene comes to life as wild horses grace a rugged land at the edge of the prairie

Painted Canyon in Dawn's Early Light

Bison grazing in Painted Canyon

Even though bison are more numerous in Yellowstone, seeing bison, here, had more meaning to me. This is home on the range where the buffalo roam and the deer and the antelope play. They seem to be more iconic, here, having once shared this wild prairie with the nations of the great plains. I became part of this scenario one evening after touring the South Unit's Scenic Loop Road. Night was falling fast as I approached the South Unit's North Boundary and the road back to Medora where I was lodging at the time. I was behind other motorists who were held up by a massive buffalo herd crisscrossing the road and grazing. This reminded me of the old west when trains were often held up for hours, and sometimes days, by mega-herds of buffalo. Still, it was a beautiful, and intriguing sight but I wanted to be back in Medora before the restaurants closed. I was quite hungry from a long day of photography exercise! It wasn't to be as it was well over an hour before I past the last few bison not making it back to my motel room until midnight. Still, in the night's darkness, I looked out the car window into frontier history.

Bison with early fall colors

In the chapter, The Great Centennial, you might remember a photo of a prairie dog, in front of a small herd of bison, in a massive prairie dog town not far from Cottonwood Campground. What I call a brotherhood, and what biologists call a symbiotic relationship, came to life in the sun's early morning glow. Prairie dogs, and their network of underground homes and entrance holes, till the ground making it rich with forage for the bison. In turn, bison fertilize the soil with their excrement (poo pies) and also till the ground with their hooves. Their grazing also keeps vegetation short making it easier for prairie dogs to see any predators in time for them to escape into their burrows. During this visit to Theodore Roosevelt National Park, I was camping at Cottonwood Campground. The evening that followed my seeing the bison in the prairie dog town, there were also bison at the campground entrance right next to Old Glory, and the entrance station, slowing down, and sometimes blocking, traffic.

Bison, and campground traffic, at the entrance of Cottonwood Campground

At the beginning of this chapter is the photo I took of the Little Missouri River meandering through Wind Canyon. Later on the same morning I photographed both the prairie dog and bison, and the wild horses on a high, treeless bluff, I arrived at the trailhead to Wind Canyon Overlook. With an overcast sky, harsh shadows would be eliminated and the landscape would stand out in full detail of its colors and shapes. As I ascended the trail, and began approaching the summit, I quickly learned how Wind Canyon received its name! It felt like a giant hand was trying to push me off the Butte. Before reaching the overlook, I was taking photos of the canyon in case I decided to turn back. The higher I ascended, the stronger the wind blew, and I could barely remain upright. Nevertheless, I did reach the summit of the overlook and was thankful there was railing to keep the wind from pushing my camera, tripod, and me off a 400-foot cliff. After finding a firm foothold, I was finally able to conserve, on film, a grand vista of Creation above me, before me, and below me, fulfilling my soul and enriching my spirit. Any sense of discomfort, and uneasiness, was replaced with a sense of awe, as though I were looking down on one of Earth's great wonders through a window in Heaven. Wind Canyon was almost the Grand Canyon in beauty and magnificence! On my way down from the overlook, below the trail in a small, thin gorge, were yellow-orange knob-shaped hoodoos so reminding me of Utah's canyon country. The hoodoo, nearest the trail, had an interesting design that, to me, looked like a short, potbellied Indian wearing an orange-topped coonskin hat. My park experience did not end with my tour of its natural beauty. In Medora, I thoroughly enjoyed visiting some its shops and eating places. The Elkhorn Café had great buffalo burger and chocolate milkshakes and, at the Badlands Pizza and Saloon, I enjoyed a roast beef dinner reminding me of old west wagon train cookouts. The Fudge and Ice Cream Depot had a great musical fruit shake reminding me of Glacier's huckleberry shakes. At the visitor center I bought, along with hats and t-shirts, the park's DVD "Refuge of The American Spirit" and a book, about our national parks, by Terry Tempest Williams, "The Hour of Land".

My only regret was not having a longer stay allowing me time to visit the Petrified Forest and the Park's North Unit, a more rugged, and forested region where bighorn sheep are found. I had to go back to work! Still, arriving at Painted Canyon Overlook and Visitor Center, before dawn, was a great last hurrah! Even in the vicinity of the visitor center, and parking lot, I could still find signs of the wild as buffalo patties were at the edge of the parking lot. Along with my camera gear, and raincoat, I had my umbrella with me not to protect me from the rain, but to protect my camera gear. A massive cloud was overhead which spanned all the way to the eastern horizon, which was clear except for a few broken clouds. The crack of dawn was grand, and surreal, as yellow, and orange light emerged from the landscape's edge, gradually filling the horizon and lighting up the edge of the storm cloud. Then came that bright yellow star atop the line of buttes, looking like it was resting upon them. From the blackness of a distant canyon glowed a small disk of light resembling a lava flow on dark rock. It was the sun's reflection but it looked like one of the sun's children lost in a sea of buttes and canyons. The massive cloud, overhead, was both a curse and a blessing. Periodic rain would have me opening up the umbrella, and holding it over the camera leaving me just one hand to position and operate the camera. Nevertheless, the cloud harmonized with the rising sun and brought forth an interspersion of soft lighting, and shadow, over the buttes and valleys before me. In the canyon, itself, even from this high overlook, I could still see a small group of wild horses and a lone bison. A new day was dawning in the beauty of God's creation!

The Wapiti Song
Music of The Greater Yellowstone

In the crisp autumn air, as aspens are aglow in gold, and bull moose pursue their cows along river shorelines, high-pitched singing rings out from mountain to mountain as a maned-neck, royal stag, with mist coming from his snout, announces his challenging of rival bulls, and summoning of royal hinds. As wild geese grace mountain-tops in their southbound flight and grizzlies graze and prey on the weak, I can hear that great melody of the wild, The Wapiti Song.

THE WAPITI SONG

Lyrics and Photography by Les MacLean

Autumn paints the mountainside and meadows with bright bold colors
V-lines of wild geese fill a red dusk sky,
In a highline meadow elk herds gather for the rigors of the mating season
And white stags raise their antlered heads up high.
A mammoth grizzly waits his turn in the shadows of a nearby glade
For a chance to kill a weakened or injured bull,
A moose family browses at the water's edge by willows of red and yellow
And dogwoods unfold in crimson bright and full.
Fiery aspens flicker in the whistling wind, mountain ash glows a pastel orange,
The white stags bugling echoes quite loud and strong,
Saber antlers clack like rifle shots in the fury of bull elk jousting
In the autumn breeze I hear the wapiti song.
To the Indians he's the wapiti, a name that means white deer,
He's an elk to the white man but to all he's noble and true,
He gathers his harem on a highline ridge and is ready to fight off rivals,
And his song rings out beneath autumn skies bright blue.
Fiery aspens flicker in the whistling wind, mountain ash glows a pastel orange,
The white stags bugling echoes quite loud and strong,
Saber antlers clack like rifle shots in the fury of bull elk jousting
In the autumn breeze I hear the wapiti song.

Trumpeter Swan on the Madison River

Bull and Cow Moose along the Yellowstone River at Sunset

On March 1, 1872, President Ulises S. Grant signed, into law, Yellowstone as the world's first national park. On February 26, 1929, Grand Teton National Park was established protecting only the mountains and several lakes at the feet of the mountains. In 1943, President Franklin D. Roosevelt declared the remaining federal land, in the Snake River Valley, as Jackson Hole National Monument. In 1949, John D. Rockefeller, Jr. donated land he purchased, 35,000 acres, to be included in the park. In 1950, the park that we know, today, was established. In 1972, the John D. Rockefeller, Jr. Memorial Parkway was established to honor his contributions to the National Park Service and our conservation legacy. Yellowstone, Grand Teton, the John D. Rockefeller Memorial Parkway, and surrounding lands are known, today, as the Greater Yellowstone Ecosystem and, to me, the home of the wapiti song since my best elk photos, including those of bulls singing, were taken here on America's Serengeti.

Mount Moran at Sunset

The land, once called "Coulter's Hell" (John Coulter the first white man known to visit the Yellowstone region), is not only famous for its geysers, hot springs, mud pots, and fumaroles, but also for its abundance of wildlife and, thanks to the reintroduction of the gray wolf in 1995, is a complete ecosystem. Grizzlies, wolves, elk, moose, bison, pronghorn, beavers, otters, eagles, trumpeter swans, and more make the Greater Yellowstone rival Africa's Serengeti and its lions, cheetahs, elephants, and wildebeests. Yellowstone, and Grand Teton, are the national parks I grew up with. My favorite time to visit this living wilderness is when the aspens are gold, the bulls of elk and moose are seeking female companionship, and when most of its visitors have returned to the city, enabling us privileged few to see this land of pristine wonder through the eyes of early explorers such as John Coulter (former member of the Lewis and Clark Expedition) and artist Thomas Moran, who was a member of the park's expedition which led to Yellowstone becoming the world's first   national park. I saw modern times, and frontier wilderness, come together when I was a part of a row of stopped vehicles when a massive buffalo herd not only crossed the roadway, but followed its course. So close was I, to these dark brown giants, I could see the hairs on their big, black nostrils, the gleam in their tiny eyes, and every curl in their wool-like fur coats. I would see bull, and cow, moose not only browsing together, but vocalizing, chasing, and sometimes, kicking one-another. But the real highlight, of my Greater Yellowstone journey, was seeing the wilderness drama unfold during the rut of these handsome, long-legged, mane-necked stags, with massive crowns of antlers, seeking hinds and fighting one-another for the right to sire next spring's calves. Their singing, and bugling, makes a wilderness symphony echoing across rivers, prairies, aspen parks, and mountaintops. This is what I call "The Wapiti Song", wapiti being their Shawnee name for the white rump patch that distinguishes them from other deer.

Bull Elk and Harem near the Mammoth Hot Springs

In one, of many, vast golden-grass meadows, a monarch bull elk (Royal-6 point on each branch Monarch-7 points per branch Imperial-8,or more, points per branch) rested not far from his harem of cows. The entire scene was soft-lit by the evening sun. It was as though a Charley Russell painting came to life! Early one morning, in a conifer-crested meadow near Jenny Lake, a lone bull elk, an imperial stag, lifted his head and sang as steam came out of his mouth. The bugling sang through my ears and filled the surrounding landscape which included the commanding back-drop of the snowclad, soft lit titan of Mount Moran. Then the songs, of other bulls, rang out from the opposite end of the landscape. Here was a land, and season, that transcended time as autumn in Greater Yellowstone came to life! I wasn't just watching this wilderness   drama, I was a part of it as all around me, countless stags, hinds, and calves were not only singing, but living the wapiti song!

Wild geese grace the Grand Teton Skyline

THE NEXT HUNDRED YEARS AND BEYOND

Bighorn ram and the Waterton Townsite Waterton Lakes National Park Alberta, Canada

PLEASE DO NOT LET THIS HAPPEN TO OUR NATION'S WILDERNESS HERITAGE!

What started here in America, in 1872, is now a world institution as there are now national parks on every continent, not just the big names such as Africa's Serengeti and Alberta, Canada's Banff, but even in such small nations as Vietnam where we were once involved in an unpopular war back in the sixties and early seventies. It is up to each and everyone of us to be wise stewards of God's blessing and America's cornerstone. We need to make better choices of who we elect as our leaders and lawmakers. We need people who care about the earth we live on and our places of physical, mental, and spiritual sanctuary. In the above photo essay, you can see what I think of our present commander n chief and his agenda which includes repealing the Environmental Protection Agency (the brainchild of another republican president Richard Nixon), removing the United States from the Paris Talks on climate change, and his desire to turn each and every U.S. national park into another Disney World. Our national parks are not for sale nor are they for the political, and economic, gain of a wealthy and privileged few. Once again, they are for the benefit and enjoyment of the people. Where we can escape the civilized rat race and share, with one-another, and the flora and fauna we share them with, as, in the immortal words of author Terry Tempest Williams, these places of inspiration, imagination, and transformation. The right decisions in our individual lives, together, can make a major, positive impact on our refuges of the American spirit, our national parks and wilderness heritage. For those who smoke, here are some online statistics to think about next time you finish smoking and decide where to discard your butt. Please use a butt container, or, after crushing out the smoke, a trash can. An estimated 1.69 billion pounds of butts wind up as toxic trash, a major burden on the environment, economy, and public health. Once discarded in the environment, they leach such toxins, as arsenic and chromium, and can be poisonous to fish and wildlife.

Fires have also been started by discarded butts so they're not just an eyesore and an environmental hazard. They are not biodegradable. On a personal note, in my present job as a custodian, when I police the grounds, and parking areas, most of the litter I pick up are cigarette butts and we even had one of our gardens catch fire. I know it's a hard thing to do, but your best decision, for your own health, and the health of both man and nature, is to stop smoking. After all, if my parents, and brother-in-law, could stop smoking, why can't you? Also, think recycling when it comes to your soda can, water bottle, or newspaper. Instead of the trash can, or "God forbid!" the environment, use a recycling container. When-ever possible, please replace driving with foot or bicycle travel. In my own day to day life, even when I still had a car, I jog to and from work, a six-mile round trip, and walk, or bike, to the library. Carpooling is also a positive alternative! Nevertheless, the next centennial, and beyond, about our national parks and overall wilderness heritage, is yours. God made these refuges, of natural and historical beauty, for us to enjoy and to steward for people yet unborn. For the next hundred years, and beyond, these wilderness parks are yours to walk the same paths, through the beauty of God's unspoiled creation, as Lewis and Clark, Sacagawea, John Muir, Theodore Roosevelt, Terry Tempest Williams, and yours's truly. To see a grizzly bear fishing for salmon or eating huckleberries, a well-crowned bull elk singing in the frosty autumn breeze, a massive buffalo herd thundering over a rolling prairie, a bighorn ram standing on the edge of Creation, or a mountain skyline graced with the soft, orange light of a morning alpenglow, is for you, and your fellow woman and man, to enjoy for Centennials to come, and for as long as the Lord shall tarry. As a blessing from God, and as an American cornerstone, our national parks, monuments, historic sites, wildlife refuges, wilderness areas, wild and scenic rivers, and even our state parks, county forest preserves, and all our natural sanctuaries, are yours and, as you act to keep them in wise stewardship, will continue to be refuges of the American and human spirit. In the Great Centennial is great healing and tranquility for one and all!

Heavenly skylines of white-threaded mountains, misty shorelines by a wave-strewn sea,

Gray wolves, grizzlies, and great buffalo herds, and icons of American history.

Arizona's great chasm carved by the Colorado, singing elk by thermals in Yellowstone,

My praise and thankfulness for the national parks, God's blessing and America's cornerstone.

Grand Teton Skyline   Grand Teton National Park

East Glacier Prairie and Skyline at Dawn   East Glacier, Montana

Barred Owl along the Cedar Run Trail Shenandoah National Park

Calypso Orchid or Fairy Slipper Glacier National Park

Lady Renee Falls Glacier National Park

BACK COVER: Lehman Caves rock formation Great Basin National Park

NATIONAL PARKS
GOD'S BLESSING AND AMERICA'S CORNERSTONE

In Glacier I witnessed a scene back in time a grizzly family walked with royalty,
a pronghorn buck stood amidst the spires of the Badlands, a Teton moose
was framed by a pine tree.
Atop a mountain I gazed upon giant cathedrals commanding vistas were filled
with ice and snow
I thanked God and Country for our national parks
where vast blue ribbon waters still flow

Heavenly skylines of white-threaded mountains, misty shorelines by a wave-strewn sea,
gray wolves, grizzlies, and great buffalo herds and icons of American history
Arizona's Great Chasm formed by the Colorado, singing elk by thermals in Yellowstone
my praise and thankfulness for the national parks,
God's Blessing and America's Cornerstone.

The parkland was born in 1872 where geysers and grizzlies make their home
Then came Muir's Yosemite, Mills' Rocky Mountain,
and the badlands where buffalo still roam,
Mather and Albright gave these lands cohesiveness
as real protection came to our parklands
Then the parks spanned from Maine's Acadia to Alaska to the Channel Islands,
Wolf re-introductions, vast wild Alaska, battlefields, and Indian cliff homes,
the parklands have gone beyond America's boundaries
to where elephants and cheetahs still roam.
As the bull elk sings to charm his hinds, the bighorn stands upon the edge of space,
I thank God for men like Grinnell, and two Roosevelts,
for preserving this wild time and place.
Roaming this land of desert castle rocks, frosty cascades, and the high Denali,
though breathless, I'm thankful for lands of majesty
where I am truly in the land of the free.

Heavenly skylines of white-threaded mountains, misty shorelines by a wave-strewn sea,
gray wolves, grizzlies, and great buffalo herds and icons of American history
Arizona's Great Chasm formed by the Colorado, singing elk by thermals in Yellowstone
my praise and thankfulness for the national parks,
God's Blessing and America's Cornerstone.

Lyrics and Photography by Les MacLean

Beaver in Cromwell Creek and autumn colors at the foot of Dorr Mountain Acadia National Park

GRIZWOLD GRIZZLY

PUBLICATIONS

www.ingramcontent.com/pod-product-compliance
Lightning Source LLC
LaVergne TN
LVHW070217080526
838202LV00067B/6839